Asia

Heather DiLorenzo Williams and Warren Rylands

EYEDISCOVER

Go to **www.eyediscover.com** and enter this book's unique code.

BOOK CODE

AVF42786

EYEDISCOVER brings you optic readalongs that support active learning.

Published by AV² by Weigl
350 5th Avenue, 59th Floor New York, NY 10118
Website: www.eyediscover.com

Library of Congress Control Number: 2018953508

ISBN 978-1-4896-8323-6 (hardcover)

Printed in the United States of America
in Brainerd, Minnesota
1 2 3 4 5 6 7 8 9 0 22 21 20 19 18

082018
120917

Project Coordinator: John Willis
Designer: Mandy Christiansen

Weigl acknowledges Alamy, iStock, and Shutterstock as the primary image suppliers for this title.

EYEDISCOVER provides enriched content, optimized for tablet use, that supplements and complements this book. EYEDISCOVER books strive to create inspired learning and engage young minds in a total learning experience.

Watch
Video content brings each page to life.

Browse
Thumbnails make navigation simple.

Read
Follow along with text on the screen.

Listen
Hear each page read aloud.

Your EYEDISCOVER Optic Readalongs come alive with...

Audio
Listen to the entire book read aloud.

Video
High resolution videos turn each spread into an optic readalong.

OPTIMIZED FOR
- TABLETS
- WHITEBOARDS
- COMPUTERS
- AND MUCH MORE!

Asia

In this book, you will learn about

- where it is
- who lives there
- what animals it has

and much more!

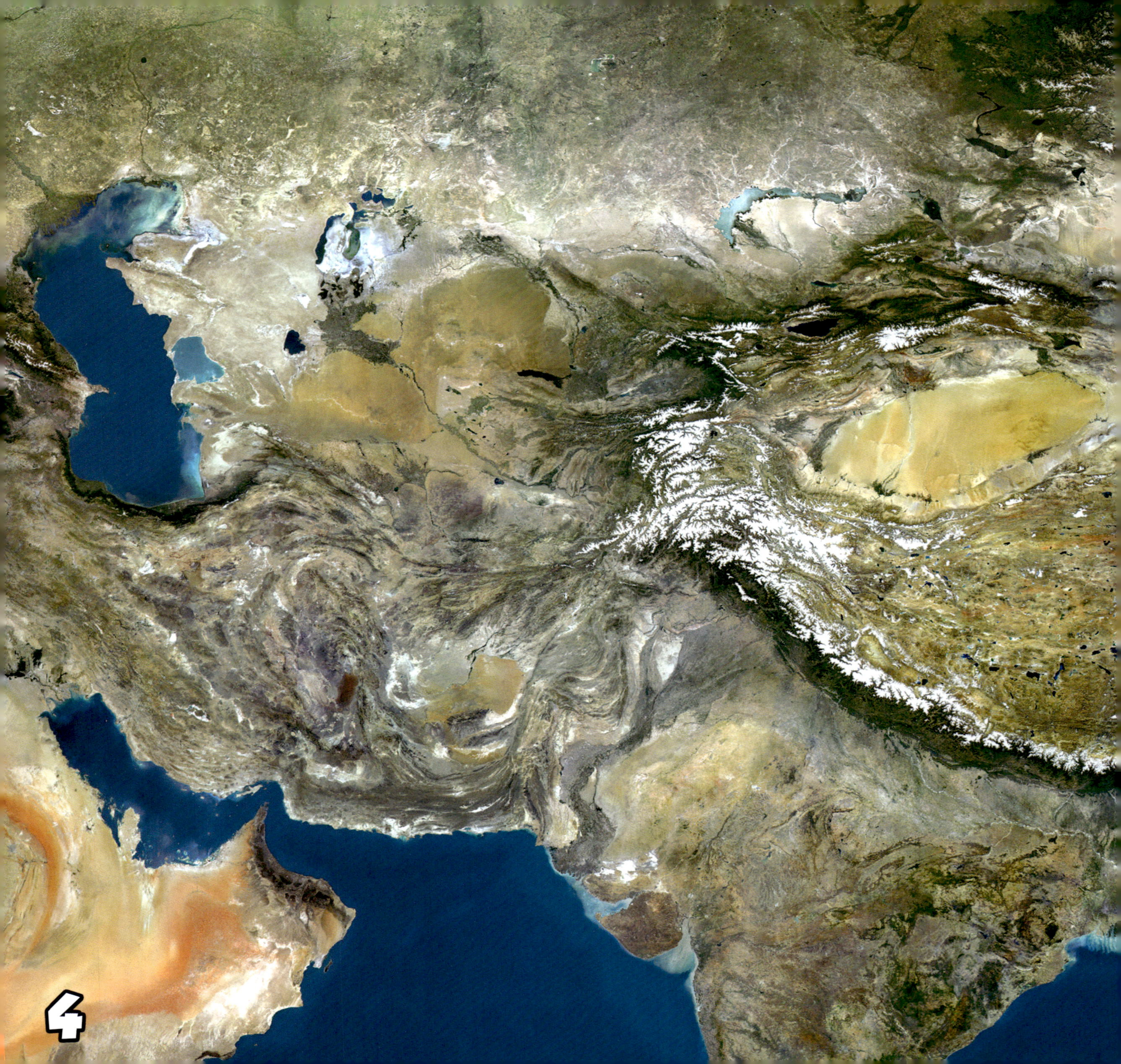
4

Asia is the largest continent on Earth. It is made up of 48 different countries.

More than 4.4 billion people live in Asia.

爱丝棋牌
上海世博会
EXPO 2010
SHANGHAI CHINA
世博门票即将向个人发售
期待...
世博热线+86-21-962010
www.expo2010.cn
志愿者招募正式启动
成功路上 知心长伴
主办：国家商务部 上海市人民政府
承办：上海跨国采购中心有限公司
您离跨国采购商

There are more people in Tokyo, Japan, than in any other Asian city.

Five of the top religions in the world started in Asia. They are Buddhism, Christianity, Hinduism, Islam, and Judaism.

12

Rice is an important food in Asia. There are more than 200 million rice farms in Asia.

Many of the world's goods are made in Asia. This includes cars, computers, and clothing.

Asia has many mountains, including Mount Everest. It is the highest mountain on Earth.

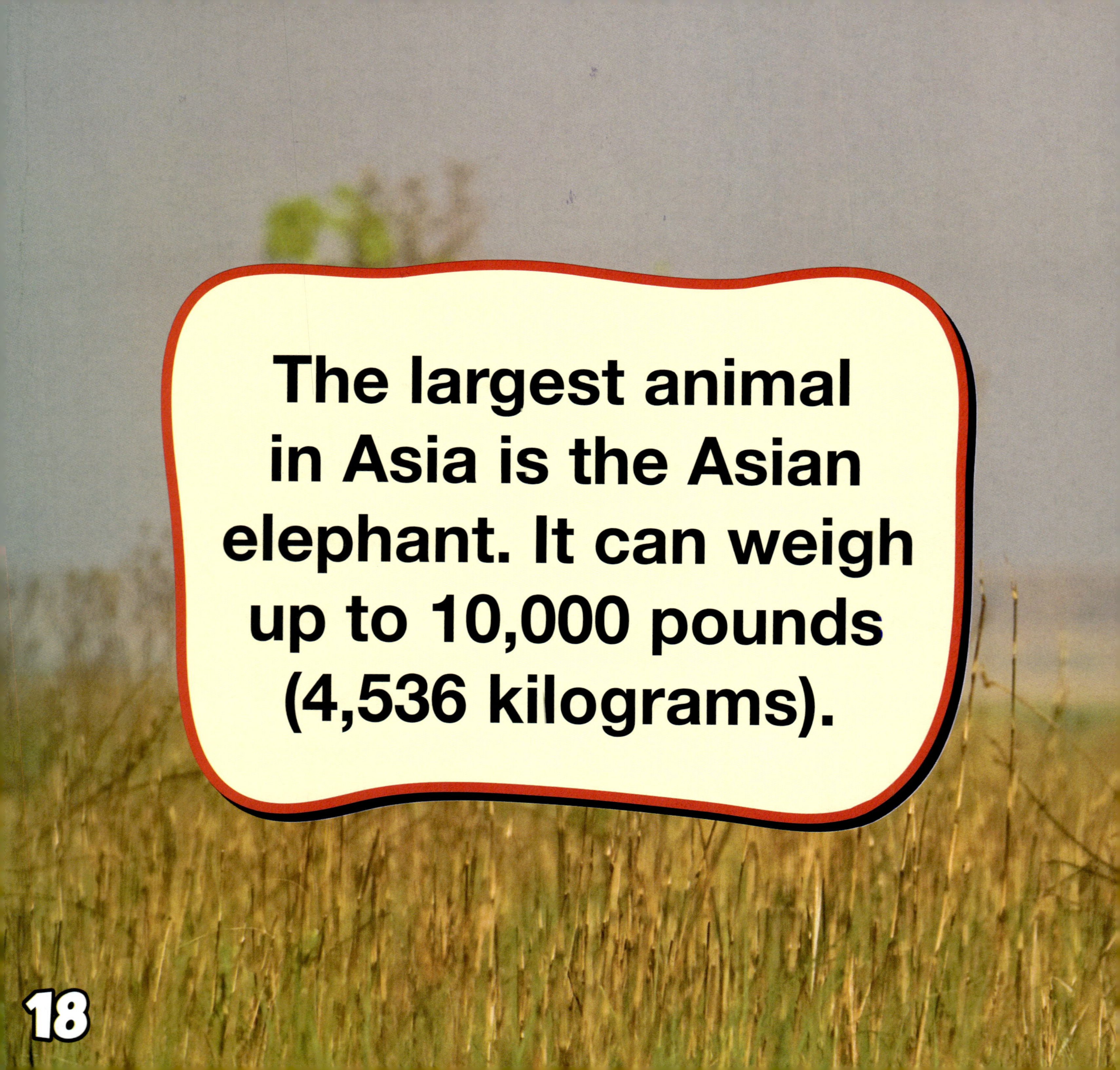

The largest animal in Asia is the Asian elephant. It can weigh up to 10,000 pounds (4,536 kilograms).

Asia is a special place with many different kinds of people, animals, and food.

ASIA BY THE NUMBERS

The Yangtze is the longest river in Asia. It is **3,964 miles** long. (6,380 kilometers)

The **smallest** country in Asia is the **Maldives**. About **440,000** people live there.

Mount Everest is **29,029 feet** tall. (8,848 meters)

In **2017**, the world's top-two most-toured cities were **Hong Kong**, China, and **Bangkok**, Thailand.

90 percent of the world's rice is grown in Asia.

More people speak **Mandarin Chinese** as their first language than any other language in the world.

KEY WORDS

Research has shown that as much as 65 percent of all written material published in English is made up of 300 words. These 300 words cannot be taught using pictures or learned by sounding them out. They must be recognized by sight. This book contains 36 common sight words to help young readers improve their reading fluency and comprehension. This book also teaches young readers several important content words, such as proper nouns. These words are paired with pictures to aid in learning and improve understanding.

Page	Sight Words First Appearance
5	different, Earth, is, it, made, of, on, the, up
6	in, live, more, people, than
9	any, are, city, other, there
10	and, started, they, world
13	an, food, important
14	many, this
17	has, mountains
18	can, to
21	a, animals, place, with

Page	Content Words First Appearance
5	Asia, continent, countries
9	city, Japan, Tokyo
10	Buddhism, Christianity, Hinduism, Islam, Judaism, religion
13	farms, rice
14	cars, clothing, computers
17	Mountains, Mount Everest
18	elephant

Watch
Video content brings each page to life.

Browse
Thumbnails make navigation simple.

Read
Follow along with text on the screen.

Listen
Hear each page read aloud.

EYEDISCOVER

Go to www.eyediscover.com and enter this book's unique code.

BOOK CODE

AVF42786